Conquering the Ocean, Discovering the Self

RAM SETU
THE BRIDGE WITHIN

BHARAT SACHDEVA

A Journey of Endurance, Faith and Unity

BookLeaf
Publishing

India | USA | UK

Presentation by *BookLeaf Publishing*

Web: www.bookleafpub.com
E-mail: info@bookleafpub.com

ISBN: 9789369546725

First edition 2025

Contents

Dedication

This book is dedicated to my dear friend Mohit Kohli—my training buddy, a true adventure enthusiast, and a noble soul.

Mohit was more than just a friend or a fellow athlete—he was a force of nature, someone whose passion for life and sport burned with an intensity few could match. He was not just an adventurer; he was a dreamer, a challenger of limits, and a man who found purpose in the pursuit of the extraordinary. Whether it was in the water, on the road, or through the mountains, he believed in testing human potential and proving that no dream was too big.

A LIFE LIVED IN MOTION

Mohit's life was one of relentless motion, and not just in the physical sense. He was always moving toward something bigger—toward new records, new horizons, and new ways to challenge himself. His last adventure, a daring attempt to cycle 10,000 km across Latin America in under 40 days, was a testament to his undying spirit. He was chasing history, setting out on a journey that demanded everything from him—grit, endurance, mental fortitude, and an unbreakable belief in himself.

Tragically, fate intervened, and his journey was cut short due to a road accident. The news sent shockwaves through our community. He was one of us—a swimmer, an adventurer, a brother in arms who thrived on pushing limits. It was impossible to process the fact that someone so full of life, so fearless, was gone in an instant.

For those of us who had trained with him, laughed with him, and shared dreams of conquering impossible challenges, his absence left a void that could never be filled. The pain of his loss was not just personal; it was collective. It was a reminder of the unpredictability of life, of how fleeting even the grandest journeys can be.

MORE THAN AN ATHLETE—A BELIEVER

Mohit was not just an athlete; he was a believer—someone who trusted existence, who surrendered himself to the journey without fear. He embraced the unknown, understanding that true adventure was not just about records or accolades but about the process, the discovery, and the sheer joy of testing oneself against nature.

There are few people who live life with such authenticity. Mohit did not just speak about big dreams—he lived them. He did not just aspire to do the impossible—he set out to do it. His mindset was simple yet profound: You either go all in or you don't go at all. And that was exactly how he approached life.

CARRYING FORWARD HIS LEGACY

Losing Mohit was a devastating reminder of how fragile life can be. But if there is one thing he would have wanted, it was for us to keep pushing, to keep chasing our own extraordinary journeys. This book, in many ways, is a reflection of that spirit.

The Ram Setu swim, though physically demanding, was never just about endurance. It was about faith, unity, and the unwavering belief that we are capable of far more than we think. That belief was something Mohit carried in every adventure he undertook. While he is no longer with us in person, his energy, his courage, and his love for testing limits live on in each of us who knew him.

We cannot bring him back, but we can honor him by continuing to challenge ourselves, embrace the unknown, and live fully, just as he did.

This book stands as a small tribute to Mohit Kohli—his dreams, his resilience, and his indomitable spirit. May his journey, though left unfinished in this world, inspire others to dream bigger, push harder, and live without fear.

Rest in power, brother. Your story continues through us.

Preface

Every great journey begins with a single, often unexpected, step—a step that propels you into uncharted territories both outside and within. Ram Setu: The Bridge Within – A Journey of Endurance, Faith, and Unity is my personal chronicle of one such journey: an expedition that was as much about traversing vast, legendary waters as it was about navigating the inner landscapes of doubt, hope, and transformation.

When the idea of swimming across Ram Setu first surfaced, it was more than a physical challenge. It was an invitation to explore the rich tapestry of history and mythology intertwined with the indomitable human spirit. Ram Setu, the ancient bridge connecting realms both literal and metaphorical, has long symbolized the triumph of determination over the seemingly insurmountable. It beckoned me to embark on a quest that promised not only to test my physical limits but also to unlock deeper reserves of courage and self-belief.

This book is a reflection of that quest. Within these pages, you will find a detailed account of the rigorous training, the moments of doubt and clarity, and the quiet victories that defined my journey across the Palk Strait. But beyond the narrative of endurance, this work is a guide—a companion for anyone seeking to overcome their own obstacles and to build bridges within themselves.

I share my story with the hope that you will find inspiration in the challenges faced and the lessons learned. It is a testament to the idea that every obstacle, no matter how formidable, is an opportunity for growth. The chapters that follow are interwoven with practical exercises, reflective prompts, and affirmations designed to help you tune into your inner wisdom and nurture your own journey of transformation.

This book would not have been possible without the unwavering support of remarkable individuals who believed in this vision. My heartfelt gratitude goes to my steadfast swim buddy on this adventure, Shaaswat Sharma, whose relentless determination, drive, and inspiring transformation ignited the spark for this expedition. I also honor the guidance and mentorship of Sucheta Debburman and the strategic support of Mr. Gaurav Bahirvani, among many others. Most poignantly, this journey is dedicated to the memory of the late Mohit Kohli—a true adventurer whose spirit continues to inspire every stroke I take.

As you delve into these pages, I invite you to see beyond the physicality of a swim. Recognize that each wave, each moment of struggle, and every surge of triumph mirror the inner battles we all face. May this book serve as both a memoir of an extraordinary challenge and a roadmap for your own journey of endurance, faith, and unity. Embrace the lessons from the bridge within, and let them guide you toward your own extraordinary horizon.

Welcome to the journey.

Introduction:
The Ocean Within

Life is like an ocean—vast, unpredictable, and filled with opportunities for discovery. Standing on the shore, staring into the unknown, we often feel the pull of something greater, a call to venture beyond our limits. But with that call comes the fear of the deep: the fear of failure, pain, and the unknown.

In 2024, I stood on a quiet beach in Sri Lanka, preparing to answer one such call. My goal was to swim across the legendary Ram Setu, the Palk Strait—a nearly 30-kilometer stretch of open water that connects Sri Lanka to India. It wasn't just a physical challenge. This journey was about more than endurance or speed; it was about bridging divides, honoring a cultural legacy, and proving to myself that human potential is limitless when we tap into our inner strength.

The journey was far from easy. I faced choppy waters, the looming fear of marine life, and mental exhaustion so intense that it felt like I couldn't take another stroke. But with every wave I overcame, I discovered something profound about life: the lessons from the ocean can guide us in every facet of our existence.

This book is about those lessons. It's about diving deep—both literally and metaphorically—into the depths of uncertainty, fear, and self-discovery. It's about building resilience, nurturing your physical and mental well-being, and finding calm in the chaos of everyday life.

Through my story, I hope to inspire you to embark on your own transformative journey. Whether it's a career change, a fitness goal, or a personal dream, you have the strength to face the waves and reach the shore.

Let this book be your guide as you navigate the ocean within.

Acknowledgments

Every great journey is built on the foundation of unwavering support, belief, and collaboration. The Ram Setu swim was more than just an expedition—it was a dream that took shape through the collective efforts of incredible individuals who stood by us, guided us, and fueled our passion.

SHAASWAT SHARMA—MY BROTHER IN ARMS

First and foremost, my deepest gratitude goes to my swimming buddy and dear friend, Shaaswat Sharma. A champion endurance athlete, Shaaswat holds the distinction of winning the 10km title at Oceanman in Phuket, eventually qualifying for the World Championship in Dubai, and later swimming in a relay split across the English Channel alongside two other phenomenal swimmers in a record time. His achievements alone speak volumes, but what makes his journey even more inspiring is the transformation he underwent to get here.

There was a time when inactivity and a lack of self-care had taken a toll on him. Yet, through sheer determination, patience, and a thoughtful approach to fitness, nutrition, and recovery, he managed to shed excess weight, gaining mobility and strength with smart, progressive planning and consistency. He rebuilt himself, one step at a time, proving that no challenge is insurmountable when the mind is set on a goal. His journey from that phase of life to becoming an elite endurance athlete is nothing short of remarkable.

Shaaswat is a living testament to perseverance—a man who, once he sets his sights on something, doesn't stop until the job is done. I am truly proud of him, not only as my partner in this adventure but also as a human being who exemplifies grit, resilience, and transformation.

It was during a casual conversation with Shaaswat that the seed for this challenge was planted. At first, I laughed at the audacity of the idea—swimming across Ram Setu, a place steeped in myth and history, seemed like an impossible feat. But as we discussed it further, we realized its true magnitude and significance. That was the turning point. It was no longer just an idea; it was a mission.

From that moment, we started taking small but meaningful steps—structuring our training, planning the logistics, and reaching out to those who could guide us in making this vision a reality. Without Shaaswat's belief, drive, and camaraderie, this journey would not have been possible.

SUCHETA DEBBURMAN—THE TRAILBLAZER

As we delved deeper into planning, we came across Sucheta Debburman, a legendary ultra-endurance swimmer and a pioneer in her own right. Sucheta holds the record of being the first Indian female swimmer to cross Ram Setu twice, a feat that is both inspiring and groundbreaking.

Her journey has empowered thousands of young girls in India to take up the sport of swimming and believe in their abilities. She has not only set records but has also led the way for future generations.

Beyond her achievements in the water, Sucheta was an invaluable mentor for us. She had already navigated the complex process of seeking permissions, coordinating with ministries, and assembling the right crew for an expedition of this scale. Her guidance and experience saved us months of effort, helping us connect with the right authorities and secure the best navigational team for our journey.

A big shoutout to Sucheta for her generosity in sharing her knowledge and for making our road to Ram Setu a little smoother. Her support was instrumental in ensuring that our expedition had the right foundation.

MR. GAURAV BAHIRVANI—THE VISIONARY CONNECTOR

Another individual who played a crucial role in making this expedition a reality is Mr. Gaurav Bahirvani, CEO of One One Six Network Limited. A bright mind in the world of fashion, entertainment, and sports management, Gaurav has worked and managed some of the biggest names in the industry.

Gaurav helped us find the perfect sponsor—**Lifelong**, a premier home and personal care brand that believed in our vision and mission. In a world where securing sponsorships for niche sports and endurance challenges is tough, Gaurav's strategic thinking and network helped us bridge that gap.

A huge thank you to **Lifelong** for coming forward to support us. Their belief in our journey and their willingness to back an expedition as unique and demanding as this gave us the resources and confidence to move forward.

TO EVERY HAND THAT HELPED

While these are the key figures who made this expedition possible, I also want to acknowledge our friends Sarthak, Etika, and Hitesh, who flew all the way from Delhi to be with us at the finish line along with Shaaswat's parents to celebrate this historic moment with us, and gratitude to all the well-wishers who stood by us throughout this journey. Whether it was through moral support, logistical assistance, training advice, or simply believing in us, every contribution mattered.

To all my fellow colleagues and the leadership team at my workplace, Step By Step School, Noida, who provided me with their full support and celebrated my accomplishments.

To the media houses that shared our story, amplifying the message of endurance, faith, and unity—thank you for helping us inspire others. Shout-out to Hero Motors, Ms. Ipshita Singh, Mr. Pankaj Dinodia, Mr. Laxmanan Shetty, Mr. Anurag Batra, and Ms. Disha Chopra for their support and encouragement.

To every individual who followed our journey, sent us words of encouragement, and believed in our ability to complete this historic swim across Ram Setu—this is for you.

This book is not just a record of an achievement. It is a testament to the power of dreams, the strength of teamwork, and the unbreakable spirit of those who dare to challenge the impossible.

With deepest gratitude,
Bharat

CHAPTER 1

Ram Setu—The Bridge of Legends

Some places are more than just geographical locations; they hold within them the weight of history, the power of myth, and the whispers of generations who have stood in awe of their presence. Ram Setu, the legendary bridge that stretches across the Palk Strait, is one such place. It is not merely a chain of limestone shoals connecting India and Sri Lanka; it is a bridge between worlds—between history and mythology, between faith and science, and between the known and the unknown.

For centuries, Ram Setu has captivated explorers, historians, and believers alike. But for me, this bridge was more than an ancient marvel—it was a symbol of endurance, faith, and unity. The idea of swimming across these waters was not just about athleticism; it was about stepping into a living legend, immersing myself in a journey that had been etched into the consciousness of an entire civilization.

THE MYTHOLOGICAL SIGNIFICANCE

The origins of Ram Setu are deeply intertwined with the epic Ramayana, one of the oldest and most revered texts

in Indian history. According to the legend, this bridge was built by Lord Rama's army of Vanaras (monkey warriors) to cross into Lanka and rescue his wife, Sita, from the demon king Ravana.

The story tells of a time when Rama, the prince of Ayodhya, stood on the shores of India, looking out at the vast ocean that separated him from his goal. Faced with an impossible challenge, he prayed to the ocean god, seeking guidance. Inspired by his unwavering faith, his devoted allies, led by the Vanara king Nala, engineered a miraculous bridge using floating stones inscribed with Rama's name.

This bridge, also called Adam's Bridge in modern times, is said to have stretched across the ocean, allowing Rama and his army to march into Lanka and fulfill their divine mission. To believers, Ram Setu is not just a physical structure—it is a testament to determination, unity, and divine intervention. It represents the idea that when faith and effort come together, even the most insurmountable obstacles can be overcome.

As a child, I had heard these stories, just as millions of others had. But standing on the shores of Sri Lanka, preparing to swim across these sacred waters, I felt their meaning in a way I never had before. I was about to traverse the same path that was once believed to have been crossed by gods and warriors.

THE HISTORICAL AND SCIENTIFIC DEBATE

Beyond mythology, Ram Setu has also been the subject of intense historical and scientific study. Some geologists and historians argue that the structure is a naturally occurring chain of limestone shoals, formed by shifting tides and geological processes over thousands of years. Others believe that it was indeed man-made, pointing to satellite images and studies that suggest a possible ancient connection between India and Sri Lanka.

The NASA satellite images of Ram Setu have fueled much debate. The bridge-like formation, stretching approximately 48 kilometers, appears distinct from the surrounding seabed. Some researchers have proposed that the structure could have been an ancient land connection, possibly used by early human civilizations to migrate between the two landmasses.

Despite these ongoing debates, one truth remains undeniable: Ram Setu has an unparalleled cultural and spiritual significance for millions. Whether seen as a divine miracle or a geological wonder, it continues to inspire awe and curiosity.

My connection to Ram Setu was not about proving its origins but about experiencing its energy—about testing my own endurance in waters that had carried the weight of myth and mystery for millennia.

THE SYMBOLISM OF RAM SETU

Ram Setu is more than just a bridge; it is a metaphor for the challenges we face in life.

- **It represents faith**—the belief that even when obstacles seem insurmountable, there is always a way forward.
- **It embodies unity**—the power of teamwork, as demonstrated by Rama and his army, who built the bridge together.
- **It symbolizes endurance**—the strength to push through limitations, both physical and mental.

As an endurance athlete, I found deep meaning in this. My journey across these waters was not just about physical stamina; it was about trusting in the process, in my training, in my team, and in something greater than myself.

Standing at the starting point of the swim, I felt the weight of history pressing upon me. This was not just another open-water swim. It was a journey through time, through legend, through the very essence of human resilience.

And so, as I took my first stroke into the waters of Ram Setu, I carried with me the same faith that had built the bridge itself—the faith that with courage, perseverance, and the right companions, any challenge could be conquered.

CHAPTER 2

The Call to Adventure

MESSAGE

Every great journey begins with the courage to say "yes."

MY STORY: THE FIRST STEP

Some ideas start as a whisper, a passing thought, a fleeting dream. Others strike like lightning, sending a jolt through your body, filling you with purpose. The idea of swimming across Ram Setu was the latter.

Shaaswat and I were in the middle of a training session when he first mentioned it. "What if we swam across Ram Setu?" he asked, his voice carrying both curiosity and excitement.

At first, I laughed. "Do you even know how far that is?"

But something, in the way he said it, stuck with me. The more I thought about it, the more it made sense. It wasn't just about the physical challenge; it was about the history, the legacy, the deeper meaning behind this stretch of water.

I spent the next few days researching. Ram Setu, also known as Adam's Bridge, is a chain of limestone shoals connecting India and Sri Lanka. According to the

Ramayana, Lord Rama's army built it to rescue Sita from the demon king Ravana. Scientists debate its origins. Some say it is a natural formation; others argue that it may have been a man-made structure. Regardless of what one believes, it remains an iconic symbol of perseverance, faith, and unity.

The more I read, the more convinced I became. This was more than just a swim. It was an opportunity to honor history, push our limits, and send a message of resilience to the world.

That night, I called Shaaswat. "Let's do it."

But over the following weeks, the idea refused to leave me. Every time I stepped into the pool or imagined the vast expanse of the Palk Strait, I felt a deep pull—a mix of excitement and fear. What if I could do it? What if this was the challenge I needed to grow, not just as a swimmer but as a person?

One evening, as I stared at the sunset over the water, I realized something profound: the greatest adventures are the ones that scare us. And so, I said, "Yes."

THE LESSONS OF THE CALL

The first step on any journey is the hardest. It's the moment when you confront your doubts, your fears, and the stories you've told yourself about what you can and cannot do.

In saying "yes" to the Ram Setu swim, I wasn't just committing to a physical challenge—I was stepping into the unknown. And that's what life often asks of us: to leave the safety of the shore and trust that we'll find our way.

INSPIRATION FOR READERS

Think about your own life. What is calling you right now? Maybe it's a career change, a fitness goal, or a creative project you've been dreaming about. Whatever it is, I want you to know this: you don't have to feel completely ready to take the first step. The courage to begin is what matters most.

PRACTICAL EXERCISE: SAYING YES TO YOUR ADVENTURE

1. **Identify Your Call**: Take a few moments to reflect on what's pulling at your heart. What is one thing you've been wanting to do but have been hesitating to start?

2. **Write It Down**: On a piece of paper or in your journal, write down the goal or challenge you want to pursue. Be specific.

3. **Make a Commitment**: Write a single sentence beginning with, "I will…" For example, "I will start training for a half-marathon" or "I will commit to writing my book."

AFFIRMATION

"I have the courage to say yes to the adventures that call me. I trust in my ability to grow through the journey."

CLOSING REFLECTION

When I stood on the shores of Sri Lanka, I didn't have all the answers. I didn't know how I'd handle the challenges ahead. But I knew one thing: I couldn't ignore the call. And neither can you.

Your journey begins the moment you choose to take the first step. Say yes, and trust that the path will reveal itself as you move forward.

CHAPTER 3

Faith, Fear, and Ocean

MESSAGE

Fear is a natural part of growth; facing it unlocks your potential.

MY STORY: FACING THE DEPTHS OF FEAR

The ocean is a paradox. It is both liberating and terrifying. It teaches you to surrender, yet it demands strength.

As someone who has spent years training in open-water swimming, I have learned to respect the sea. You never conquer it; you only learn to move with it.

But this swim was different. It was longer, riskier, and filled with unknowns. What if the currents were too strong? What if exhaustion sets in too early? What if something went wrong mid-swim?

What if I failed? What if I wasn't strong enough to overcome the tides, the exhaustion, or the relentless uncertainty? Worse still, what if the sea itself turned against me? Stories of jellyfish stings, sharks, and unseen dangers lurking beneath the surface played in my mind.

The night before the swim, I couldn't sleep. My mind raced with every possible scenario, most of them ending

in failure. But as the morning sun rose, I reminded myself why I was here. This was about more than me—it was about proving that fear doesn't have to define us. With every stroke I took, I chose to move through the fear instead of away from it.

These fears crept in during our training sessions. We had to learn to push past them. The only way to truly prepare for an open-water endurance swim is to become one with the water, to move in harmony with the waves, to trust your body, and to believe that you can finish.

Fear is natural, but faith is a choice. And we were choosing faith.

THE NATURE OF FEAR

Fear is an instinct designed to protect us, but too often, it becomes a barrier that holds us back. Whether it's fear of failure, rejection, or the unknown, it whispers, "Stay where you are. It's safer here."

But fear is also a sign that you're on the edge of growth. The very things we're afraid of are often the gateways to our greatest achievements. The key is learning to embrace fear as a guide rather than a roadblock.

INSPIRATION FOR READERS

Think about a goal or dream that excites you but also scares you. That fear is a sign that it matters to you. Instead of letting it paralyze you, use it as fuel. Remember, fear is not your enemy—it's your teacher.

PRACTICAL EXERCISES: TRANSFORMING FEAR INTO ACTION

1. **Name Your Fear**: Write down what you're afraid of. Be specific. For example, "I'm afraid of failing at X because…"
2. **Reframe the Fear**: Next to each fear, write down how facing it could benefit you. For example, "If I face this fear, I'll grow stronger, more confident, or more resilient."
3. **Take a Small Step**: Commit to one small action that brings you closer to your goal, even if it feels uncomfortable.

AFFIRMATION

"I acknowledge my fears, but they do not control me. I face them with courage and grow stronger with each step."

CLOSING REFLECTION

Fear will always be a part of life's journey, but it doesn't have to steer the ship. Each time you face it, you reclaim your power. Remember, the greatest adventures often lie on the other side of fear.

CHAPTER 4

Resilience in the Face of Obstacles

MESSAGE

True resilience is built in the moments when giving up feels easier than moving forward.

MY STORY: PUSHING THROUGH THE STORM

At the halfway point of the Ram Setu swim, I hit a wall—physically, mentally, and emotionally. The waves had grown more unpredictable, and I found myself fighting against currents that seemed determined to push me back. My muscles burned; my breathing grew labored due to lack of sleep on the boat a night prior and motion sickness. I vomited multiple times, and every stroke felt heavier than the last.

The thought of quitting crept into my mind. "No one would blame you," I told myself. "You've already come so far." But deep down, I knew I couldn't stop. Quitting wasn't an option—not because of external expectations, but because I had promised myself that I would finish.

I focused on the immediate task: one stroke, then another. I tuned out the pain and kept my mind anchored

in the present moment. Slowly but surely, I found my rhythm again. The storm inside me calmed, and I pressed on toward the shore.

THE NATURE OF RESILIENCE

Resilience isn't about never struggling; it's about continuing to move forward despite the struggle. It's built in the moments when you feel like giving up but choose to persist.

Life is full of storms—unexpected challenges, setbacks, and moments of self-doubt. Resilience doesn't eliminate these obstacles, but it gives you the strength to weather them and emerge stronger on the other side.

INSPIRATION FOR READERS

Think about a challenge you're facing right now. What would it look like to meet it with resilience? Remember, resilience is not about perfection. It's about persistence.

PRACTICAL EXERCISES: BUILDING RESILIENCE

1. **Focus on the Present**: When challenges feel overwhelming, break them down into smaller, manageable steps. Ask yourself, "What's the next right thing I can do?"
2. **Reflect on Past Wins**: Recall a time when you overcame a difficult situation. What helped you succeed? Use that experience as a reminder of your strength.
3. **Practice Self-Compassion**: Treat yourself with kindness when things get tough. Resilience grows when you acknowledge your efforts and progress.

AFFIRMATION

"I am resilient. With each challenge I face, I grow stronger and more capable."

CLOSING REFLECTION

Resilience is like a muscle: the more you use it, the stronger it becomes. Every obstacle you face is an opportunity to build that strength. Remember, the storm may rage, but you have the power to endure.

CHAPTER 5

The Power of Community and Connection

MESSAGE

No journey is truly solitary; we thrive when we support and uplift one another.

MY STORY: STRENGTH IN NUMBERS

During the Ram Setu swim, there were moments when I felt utterly alone. The vastness of the ocean stretched endlessly around me, and the silence was deafening. But then, I would catch sight of Shaaswat and the support boats nearby, hear the cheers of my team, or think of the people who believed in me.

Their encouragement reminded me that I wasn't swimming just for myself. My journey was about something bigger—bridging divides, inspiring others, and showing what's possible when we come together.

Even when I felt like I couldn't take another stroke, the strength of my community lifted me. Their belief in me reignited my belief in myself.

THE IMPORTANCE OF CONNECTION

Human beings are wired for connection. Whether we're pursuing a personal goal or navigating life's challenges, the support of others can make all the difference. Community provides encouragement, accountability, and a sense of belonging.

No matter how independent you are, remember this: you don't have to do it all alone.

INSPIRATION FOR READERS

Who is in your corner? Think about the people who uplift and inspire you. And just as importantly, ask yourself how you can be that person for someone else.

PRACTICAL EXERCISES: STRENGTHENING YOUR COMMUNITY

1. **Reach Out**: Identify one person who inspires you or shares your goals. Schedule time to connect with them and exchange ideas or support.

2. **Offer Support**: Think of someone who might need encouragement right now. Send them a message or offer to help in a small but meaningful way.
3. **Build a Tribe**: Join a group or community that aligns with your interests or goals, whether it's fitness, personal development, or a creative pursuit.

AFFIRMATION

"I am surrounded by a supportive community that uplifts and inspires me. Together, we are stronger."

CLOSING REFLECTION

Community is the foundation of every great journey. When we connect with others, we share strength, multiply joy, and divide burdens. Remember, no matter how vast the ocean may seem, you are never truly alone.

CHAPTER 6

The Balance Between Effort and Rest

MESSAGE

Growth happens in the balance between action and recovery.

MY STORY: LISTENING TO THE OCEAN AND MY BODY

Training for the Ram Setu swim taught me the value of pushing my limits—but it also taught me the importance of knowing when to stop. There were days when I felt invincible, clocking long hours in the water and pushing my body to adapt to the demands of open-water swimming. But there were also days when exhaustion crept in, and my body begged for rest.

In the early stages of training, I ignored those signals. I believed that more effort equaled more results. But I soon discovered the dangers of overtraining—fatigue, injuries, and a loss of motivation. I realized that rest wasn't a sign of weakness; it was a necessary part of growth.

On the day of the swim, this balance was crucial. I paced myself, alternating bursts of power with moments

of steady rhythm. I tuned into my body and adjusted my effort accordingly. That balance between effort and rest carried me through the toughest stretches of the journey.

THE IMPORTANCE OF BALANCE

In life, as in training, balance is everything. Too much effort without rest leads to burnout. Too much rest without effort leads to stagnation. Growth happens when we honor both sides of the equation.

Rest is not just about physical recovery—it's about mental and emotional renewal. It's in the stillness that we regain clarity, process our experiences, and prepare for what's next.

INSPIRATION FOR READERS

Are you honoring the balance between effort and rest in your life? Consider where you might be overextending yourself or, conversely, where you might be holding back. Strive for a rhythm that supports both growth and renewal.

PRACTICAL EXERCISES: FINDING YOUR BALANCE

1. **Schedule Rest Days**: Whether it's in your fitness routine or daily life, plan intentional days for rest and recovery. Use this time to recharge.
2. **Practice Active Rest**: Engage in activities that rejuvenate you, such as yoga, meditation, or a leisurely walk in nature.
3. **Reflect on Your Energy Levels**: At the end of each day, ask yourself: "Did I give too much or too little today? How can I find a better balance tomorrow?"

AFFIRMATION

"I honor the balance between effort and rest. Both are essential for my growth and well-being."

CLOSING REFLECTION

Balance is not about perfection; it's about harmony. When you embrace both effort and rest, you create space for sustainable growth and lasting transformation.

CHAPTER 7

Gratitude and the Power of Reflection

MESSAGE

Gratitude transforms the way we see our journey, and reflection helps us grow from it.

MY STORY: A MOMENT OF GRATITUDE AT THE FINISH LINE

As I emerged from the waters of the Ram Setu swim, the cheers of the crowd filled the air. My body was exhausted, but my spirit was alive with a sense of accomplishment. I took a moment to look back at the ocean, a silent witness to my journey.

I thought about everything that had brought me to this point—the months of training, the challenges I had faced, and the people who had supported me along the way. Gratitude swelled in my heart. I realized that this wasn't just a personal achievement; it was a collective victory.

Later that evening, as I reflected on the experience, after a heart touching surprise celebration with our friends, I wrote down everything I was grateful for—the strength

of my body, the resilience of my mind, the beauty of the ocean, and the power of human connection. That simple act of reflection deepened my sense of fulfillment and taught me the importance of pausing to acknowledge life's gifts.

THE POWER OF GRATITUDE

Gratitude shifts our focus from what we lack to what we have. It's a practice that fosters positivity, resilience, and a deeper connection to life.

Reflection, on the other hand, allows us to learn from our experiences. By looking back, we gain clarity, recognize patterns, and uncover the lessons hidden in our journey. Together, gratitude and reflection create a powerful foundation for growth.

INSPIRATION FOR READERS

What are you grateful for today? Take a moment to reflect on your journey so far—its challenges, its triumphs, and the lessons it has taught you. Gratitude and reflection can transform the way you see your life.

PRACTICAL EXERCISES: CULTIVATING GRATITUDE AND REFLECTION

1. **Start a Gratitude Journal**: Write down three things you're grateful for each day, no matter how small.
2. **Set Reflection Time**: At the end of each week, spend 10 minutes reflecting on what went well, what challenged you, and what you learned.
3. **Express Gratitude**: Reach out to someone who has positively impacted your life and let them know how much you appreciate them.

AFFIRMATION

"I embrace gratitude and reflection as tools for growth and joy. My journey is full of gifts and lessons."

CLOSING REFLECTION

Gratitude and reflection are the keys to unlocking the beauty of your journey. When you pause to appreciate and learn from your experiences, you pave the way for even greater growth and fulfillment.

CHAPTER 8

The Role of Intuition and Inner Strength

MESSAGE

Your intuition is a compass, guiding you toward your true potential, while inner strength helps you stay the course.

MY STORY: TRUSTING MY INNER VOICE

As I swam through the vast expanse of the Palk Strait, there were moments of doubt and uncertainty. Was I pacing myself correctly? Could my body endure the hours ahead? Should I adjust my course? In those moments, I had to rely on something deeper than physical preparation or external feedback: my intuition.

I had trained my body to navigate the unpredictable ocean, but I had also trained my mind to trust its instincts. When I felt the currents shift, I adjusted my stroke without overthinking. When fatigue set in, I listened to my inner voice urging me forward. This wasn't blind determination—it was a dialogue with my intuition, a trust in the wisdom I had cultivated through experience.

Looking back, I realized that trusting my intuition was one of the most empowering aspects of the journey.

It reminded me that we often have the answers we seek within us; we just need the courage to listen.

THE ROLE OF INTUITION

Intuition is the quiet voice of your inner wisdom. It's not impulsive or reckless; it's a deep knowing that comes from experience, self-awareness, and connection to your values.

Inner strength, on the other hand, is the resilience and courage to act on that intuition, even when fear or doubt creeps in. Together, they form the foundation of confident decision-making and authentic living.

INSPIRATION FOR READERS

Think about a decision or challenge you're currently facing. What is your intuition telling you? Are you giving yourself the space to listen? Remember, your inner strength grows each time you trust and act on your inner voice.

PRACTICAL EXERCISES: CULTIVATING INTUITION AND INNER STRENGTH

1. **Quiet the Noise**: Spend 5-10 minutes each day in silence or meditation to tune into your thoughts and feelings.
2. **Trust Small Decisions**: Practice listening to your intuition in everyday situations—choosing a path during a walk, deciding how to spend your day, or responding to a challenge.
3. **Strengthen Your Core Values**: Write down what matters most to you. Use these values as a guide to make decisions that align with your authentic self.

AFFIRMATION

"I trust my intuition and draw strength from within. I have the wisdom to navigate my journey."

CLOSING REFLECTION

Your intuition is a gift ,and your inner strength is its ally. Together ,they empower you to face uncertainties with confidence and clarity.

CHAPTER 9

The Day of Reckoning

MESSAGE

The Day of Reckoning is the moment when every ounce of training, every hour of preparation, and every seed of inner strength is put to the ultimate test. It is the day when theory meets reality, and you must stand face to face with the challenge that you've been preparing for. This is not merely a physical test—it is a profound moment of truth where your determination, resilience, and self-belief are fully revealed.

MY STORY: CONFRONTING THE ULTIMATE TEST

I woke before dawn, the air crisp and heavy with anticipation. The night on the boat was long, restless, filled with quiet reflections and a mix of excitement and anxiety. On that morning, as I stood on the boat near the shoreline of Talaimannar, every element around me—the soft murmur of the sea, the first pale hints of sunrise, and the steady support of my team—reminded me of the journey that had led to this pivotal moment.

I recall the final moments before the plunge with
Shaaswat vividly. I checked my gear one last time, my body
smeared with grease to ward off any sea creature, my heart
pounding in tandem with the rhythmic lapping of the
waves. Every training session, every early morning swim,

and every ounce of mental preparation had culminated in that singular moment. Doubt and fear hovered at the edges of my mind, but I also felt an overwhelming sense of readiness. This was my day of reckoning—a time to let go of what-ifs and embrace the reality of my challenge head-on.

As I took the first stroke into the vast, open water, I felt both the weight of the unknown and the empowering rush of purpose. The currents tested me immediately; their unpredictable force a stark reminder of nature's might. Yet, with every pull of my arms and every synchronized kick, I felt my inner strength surge. I was not merely fighting the physical distance; I was engaging in a deeper dialogue with myself, confronting every fear and every limitation that had once seemed insurmountable.

THE ROLE OF PREPARATION AND INNER GUIDANCE

The Day of Reckoning is where meticulous preparation meets the unpredictable pulse of reality. All the hours spent refining my technique, building endurance, and nurturing my inner voice coalesced in this moment. It was here that I realized the true value of trusting my intuition. When the waves grew tumultuous and fatigue began to whisper its doubts, it was that inner compass—honed by months of disciplined training—that guided my every move. I learned to listen to my body's subtle signals, adjusting my pace and stroke to navigate the challenges as they came.

This interplay of rigorous preparation and intuitive decision-making became my lifeline. It allowed me to transform the fear of the unknown into a wellspring of strength and clarity. In the chaos of the open water, where every second was both a battle and a revelation, I discovered that the most potent tool I had was my unwavering belief in myself.

INSPIRATION FOR READERS

Your own Day of Reckoning might not involve vast oceans or physical endurance, but it is no less significant. Each of us faces moments when our preparedness and inner resolve are tested—be it in our careers, relationships, or personal endeavors. Reflect on a time when you had to confront a challenge head-on. What did you learn from that experience? How did it change your perspective on your own strengths?

Embrace your moments of reckoning as opportunities to rediscover your resilience. Every challenge is a doorway to personal growth, a chance to prove to yourself that you can overcome even the most daunting obstacles. Remember, the true test lies not in the absence of fear but in the courage to act despite it.

PRACTICAL EXERCISES: PREPARING FOR YOUR DAY OF RECKONING

1. **Visualization:**
   - Spend a few minutes each day imagining yourself in a challenging situation. Visualize the obstacles

in detail, and then see yourself navigating through them with calm determination and strategic action.

2. **Mindfulness Meditation:**
   - Dedicate 10 minutes daily to mindfulness meditation. Focus on your breath and allow your thoughts to settle. This practice can help you center yourself so you're better equipped to face unexpected challenges.

3. **Reflective Journaling:**
   - Write about a recent challenge or an upcoming one. Describe your feelings, the resources you can draw upon, and the steps you plan to take. Reviewing your reflections over time can help build confidence in your ability to face future days of reckoning.

4. **Affirmation Practice:**
   - Develop a personal mantra that resonates with your inner strength. Repeat it each morning to set a confident tone for the day ahead.

AFFIRMATION

"Today, I embrace my challenge. I trust in my preparation and my inner strength. I am ready to face the unknown, for I know that every step I take brings me closer to my true potential."

CLOSING REFLECTION

The Day of Reckoning is a powerful reminder that life's greatest lessons often come at the moment when we are forced to confront our deepest fears and uncertainties. It is in these moments that the sum of our efforts and our inner fortitude shines brightest. As you prepare for your own challenges, know that every step taken in the face of adversity builds a stronger, wiser, and more resilient you.

Let your Day of Reckoning be a celebration of your courage—a day when you choose to transform fear into action, uncertainty into clarity, and challenges into triumphs. Embrace this moment as a stepping stone toward a future where every obstacle is an opportunity for growth and every challenge a testament to your inner power.

CHAPTER 10

Reaching the Other Side

MESSAGE

Reaching the other side is not merely about completing a physical journey—it's about crossing a threshold into a new state of being. This chapter celebrates the moment when determination and inner strength converge to transform struggle into triumph, marking the end of one chapter and the exciting beginning of another.

MY STORY: THE MOMENT OF ARRIVAL

I vividly remember the instant I saw the distant shoreline of Dhanushkodi emerge from the horizon. After hours of battling relentless currents, fatigue, and the weight of self-doubt, every ounce of training and every whispered affirmation coalesced into that singular moment of clarity. As I propelled myself through the water, my senses sharpened—the rhythm of my strokes, the cool embrace of the ocean, and the distant murmur of voices on land all signified that the finish was near.

In those final moments, every hardship I'd encountered transformed into a profound sense of gratitude. I realized that reaching the other side was not just about finishing a

swim; it was about embracing the journey that reshaped my understanding of perseverance, self-belief, and the inexhaustible capacity for change. That moment was a culmination of countless early mornings, moments of solitude in the water, and the steady support of everyone who believed in this vision. It was a silent celebration of both a victory over external obstacles and an inner transformation that would forever alter the way I saw myself.

THE ROLE OF COMPLETION AND NEW BEGINNINGS

Crossing over to the other side served as a powerful metaphor for personal evolution. It wasn't simply an end, but a profound beginning. The physical act of emerging from the water into a new land mirrored the internal journey—from doubt to clarity, from struggle to strength. Reaching the other side affirmed that every challenge faced and every barrier overcome had prepared me for this transformative moment. The finish line was a testament to the idea that our deepest trials often lead to our most significant breakthroughs.

This milestone encouraged me to reflect on the bridge between our past and our potential. It taught me that every drop of sweat, every moment of fear, and every burst of energy was not in vain—they were the building blocks of a stronger, more resilient self. That day, I understood that achieving a goal is not the final destination; rather, it is a springboard that launches us into new adventures and a renewed commitment to pursue even greater dreams.

INSPIRATION FOR READERS

To those reading this, reaching your own "other side" might look very different—perhaps it's overcoming a long-standing challenge, achieving a career milestone, or finding inner peace after a turbulent period. The essence is the same: when you persist, when you trust in your training—both physical and mental—you unlock new realms of possibility.

Ask yourself: What is the "other side" of your current challenge? What personal barrier are you ready to overcome? Let my journey remind you that each step, no matter how small, is a powerful act of progress. Embrace the idea that every challenge is not a dead end but a door opening to new opportunities.

PRACTICAL EXERCISES: CELEBRATING YOUR JOURNEY FORWARD

1. **Milestone Mapping**: Write down a significant challenge you've overcome. Reflect on the steps you took and the lessons learned along the way. Recognize this as a milestone on your journey to the next phase of your life.

2. **Visualization of Success**: Dedicate a few minutes daily to visualize yourself achieving your goals. Picture the moment you "reach the other side" of your personal challenge, and feel the emotions associated with that triumph.

3. **Gratitude Journaling**: Keep a daily journal where you note at least one thing you are grateful for in your journey. Recognize that every effort, every struggle, and every victory is a building block for future success.

4. **Celebratory Ritual:** Create a personal ritual to mark significant achievements. This could be as simple as a quiet moment of reflection, a walk in nature, or sharing your success with someone who has supported you along the way.

AFFIRMATION

"I have crossed the threshold of challenge and emerged stronger. Every step I take brings me closer to my true potential, and every finish is the start of a new journey."

CLOSING REFLECTION

Reaching the other side is a reminder that every journey, no matter how arduous, carries within it the promise of transformation. It is a moment to pause, celebrate, and then courageously step into the next phase of your life with renewed energy and purpose. As you reflect on your own path, remember that the finish line is not an end—it's a powerful beginning. Embrace your achievements, learn from your experiences, and step forward with confidence into a future full of endless possibilities.

CHAPTER 11

Lessons from the Bridge Within

MESSAGE

This chapter is about recognizing that the true journey isn't just across the physical expanse of water—it's the internal crossing from doubt to clarity, from fear to empowerment. The "bridge within" represents the transformative path where challenges are met with self-awareness, resilience, and a deep trust in our inner wisdom.

MY STORY: CROSSING THE INNER BRIDGE

During the most grueling moments of my Ram Setu swim, I came to understand that the true challenge lay not in the physical distance but in the inner battle I waged with every stroke. As I navigated the shifting currents and unpredictable tides, I began to see parallels between the ocean's vastness and the uncharted territories within my own mind.

In the early hours of my swim, when every muscle screamed in protest and the horizon seemed infinitely distant, I felt a wave of despair. Yet, amid the pounding of

the surf and the relentless push of fatigue, I discovered a quiet space within—a moment of stillness where my inner voice spoke with clarity. It was in this space that I found the courage to persist, drawing strength from memories of every small victory along the way. I realized that each stroke was not just a physical effort but a symbolic step across a bridge that connected my past fears to my future potential.

As the journey unfolded, the boundaries between the external challenge and my inner world blurred. Every surge of energy and every moment of surrender was a lesson: that the bridge within, built through self-belief and introspection, was just as vital as the bridge of stone and legend that spanned the Palk Strait.

THE ROLE OF INTUITION AND INNER AWARENESS

The "bridge within" is constructed through our ability to listen to our inner self. Intuition in this context is the quiet guidance that helps you navigate life's uncertainties. It is not merely an instinctive reaction but a refined understanding of your own strengths, fears, and potential.

In my swim, there were moments when logic and training could not answer every question. Instead, I had to rely on that inner compass to adjust my pace, alter my course, and make split-second decisions that kept me aligned with my purpose. Inner awareness allowed me to discern when to push forward and when to conserve energy—a subtle interplay of mind and body that transcended physical endurance. This internal dialogue was as transformative as the swim itself, forging a bridge that connected my deepest vulnerabilities with newfound strengths.

INSPIRATION FOR READERS

I invite you to reflect on your own "bridge within." Consider the challenges you face—be they professional, personal, or emotional—and ask yourself: What internal resources have you yet to fully explore? Perhaps you've been held back by self-doubt or the fear of failure. Just as I discovered hidden reserves of strength while swimming through turbulent waters, you, too, can unlock potential by trusting in your inner wisdom.

Remember, every obstacle you overcome builds that inner bridge, enabling you to move from a place of uncertainty to one of confidence and clarity. Your journey, regardless of how daunting it may seem, is a powerful testament to your ability to grow and transform.

PRACTICAL EXERCISES: BUILDING YOUR INNER BRIDGE

1. **Meditative Reflection:** Dedicate 10 minutes each day to quiet meditation. Focus on your breathing and let your thoughts settle. In this stillness, notice any intuitive insights that arise.

2. **Journaling Your Journey:** Write about a recent challenge you faced. Reflect on how you responded—what emotions surfaced, and what inner guidance did you notice? Over time, this practice will help you identify patterns and build trust in your inner voice.

3. **Visualizing Success:** Imagine a bridge within yourself that spans from where you are today to where you aspire to be. Visualize each plank as a skill, value, or insight that supports your journey. This exercise helps solidify the connection between your current challenges and your future achievements.

4. **Affirmative Actions:** Identify one small decision each day where you can act on your intuition. It might be choosing a healthier meal, taking a different route that feels right, or simply listening more intently during a conversation. Celebrate these moments as steps toward building a resilient inner bridge.

AFFIRMATION

"I embrace the journey within. My inner voice is my guide, and every challenge I overcome strengthens the bridge to my true potential."

CLOSING REFLECTION

The lessons from the "bridge within" remind us that true growth comes from within. Just as I learned to trust my instincts and overcome the physical challenges of the swim, you are invited to embark on your own internal journey. In doing so, you will discover that the strength to face external challenges lies in the quiet power of your inner world.

Embrace your inner journey with the knowledge that every step—no matter how small—is a step toward a stronger, wiser, and more authentic you. Your inner bridge is waiting to be built, one thoughtful decision at a time.

CHAPTER 12

Carrying the Legacy Forward

MESSAGE

A journey of such magnitude does not end with a single accomplishment—it creates ripples that extend far beyond the individual. Carrying the legacy forward means sharing the lessons learned, inspiring others to chase their dreams, and using our experiences as a beacon of hope and resilience.

MY STORY: PASSING ON THE TORCH

After reaching the far shore, I realized that the impact of my journey was not confined to the hours spent in open water. In the quiet aftermath, as I reflected on each grueling moment and every triumph, I understood that the story of Ram Setu was as much about community as it was about personal achievement. I began to share my experiences with fellow athletes, aspiring swimmers, and anyone grappling with their own challenges. The encouragement I received in return was overwhelming—each person found a spark of inspiration to overcome

their own barriers in my story. This mutual exchange of hope and resilience reinforced the idea that our individual journeys, when shared, create a collective legacy of courage and transformation.

LEARNING FOR READERS

- **Inspiration**: Recognize that your experiences, however personal, have the power to inspire others.

- **Community**: Understand the value of sharing your story as a way to build connections and foster collective growth.
- **Empowerment**: Embrace the responsibility to carry forward the lessons learned, turning personal victories into communal progress.

PRACTICAL EXERCISES: SHARING YOUR JOURNEY

1. **Storytelling Sessions**: Organize a small gathering or join an online forum where you can share your personal challenges and triumphs.
2. **Mentorship**: Offer guidance to someone facing similar obstacles. Sharing your insights can empower both you and the person you help.
3. **Creative Expression**: Write a blog, create a video, or even start a journal that chronicles your journey. Let your experiences serve as a roadmap for others in search of hope and direction.

AFFIRMATION

"I honor my journey by sharing its lessons. My story is a beacon of resilience, inspiring others to believe in the power of transformation."

CLOSING REFLECTION

Carrying the legacy forward is about more than just recounting past victories—it's about lighting the way for others to follow. As you share your journey, remember that each act of vulnerability and courage has the potential to spark a movement of hope. Your legacy is a living testament to the transformative power of perseverance, destined to inspire future generations.

CHAPTER 13

Embracing a New Beginning

MESSAGE

Every ending is merely a prelude to a new beginning. As we close one chapter, we open the door to endless possibilities—new challenges, fresh opportunities, and the chance to continually redefine our limits. Embracing a new beginning is about recognizing that the journey never truly ends; it evolves.

MY STORY: THE DAWN OF A NEW ADVENTURE

Standing on the shore of Dhanushkodi after my historic swim with Shaaswat, I felt a profound sense of closure mingled with the excitement of new possibilities. The physical exhaustion gave way to a serene clarity—a realization that while the swim marked the end of one epic challenge, it was also the beginning of a transformative phase in my life. I began to see the world through a different lens, one where every challenge was an opportunity to evolve and every ending set the stage for a bold new adventure. In that moment, I promised

myself that I would not let the thrill of this achievement be a final destination but rather a stepping stone toward even greater pursuits.

LEARNING FOR READERS

- **Transformation**: Recognize that every major achievement is a gateway to further growth and exploration.
- **Openness**: Embrace new beginnings with an open heart and mind, ready to face fresh challenges.
- **Continuous Evolution**: Understand that the journey of self-improvement and discovery is never truly complete—it is an ongoing process of renewal.

PRACTICAL EXERCISES: CHARTING YOUR NEW COURSE

1. **Goal Setting**: Reflect on your recent accomplishments and outline new goals that excite and challenge you.

Write them down and create a roadmap for achieving these dreams.

2. **Vision Board**: Craft a visual representation of your future aspirations. Include images, quotes, and symbols that resonate with your new beginnings.
3. **Daily Reflection**: At the end of each day, take a few minutes to reflect on what you learned and how it can propel you toward your next adventure.

AFFIRMATION

"I embrace every ending as the start of a new journey. I am open to the endless possibilities that lie ahead, and I trust that each new challenge will reveal my untapped potential."

CLOSING REFLECTION

Embracing a new beginning means recognizing that the journey of life is an ever-evolving story. With every closing chapter, we gain the wisdom and strength to start afresh, ready to conquer new horizons. Let the end of this expedition be a reminder that your potential is boundless, and every new dawn offers a chance to redefine what's possible. Step forward with courage, knowing that the future is a canvas waiting to be painted with your dreams.

CHAPTER 14

The Echoes of the Journey

MESSAGE

Long after the physical journey ends, the echoes of our experiences continue to resonate within us and our communities. This chapter explores how the lessons learned and the inner transformations achieved reverberate through our lives, influencing future decisions, shaping our character, and inspiring those around us.

MY STORY: THE LINGERING RESONANCE

After stepping onto the shore and celebrating the triumph of reaching the other side, I found that the end of my swim was not a conclusion but the beginning of a profound internal evolution. In the quiet moments that followed, I noticed how the lessons of endurance, faith, and unity had seeped into every aspect of my life. Every decision, every challenge thereafter, was imbued with a new clarity and humility—a reminder of the powerful transformation I had undergone.

In daily interactions and quiet reflections, I could still hear the echoes of that monumental journey: the rhythm of the ocean in my heartbeat, the persistent call of my

inner voice guiding me during tough times, and the deep gratitude for every moment of struggle that had led to my growth. These echoes not only shaped my own path but also became a source of inspiration for friends, family, and aspiring athletes who saw in my story the potential for their own transformation.

THE ROLE OF RESONANCE IN TRANSFORMATION

The echoes of our journey act as silent mentors that continue to whisper wisdom even when the physical challenge is over. They remind us of our resilience, encourage us to trust our instincts, and empower us to face future uncertainties with confidence. This resonance is not merely nostalgic; it is a living force that continuously nurtures our inner strength and informs our actions. It compels us to share our experiences, creating a ripple effect that empowers others to embark on their own quests for self-discovery and growth.

INSPIRATION FOR READERS

Consider how the lessons from your own challenges continue to shape you. What echoes from past struggles still guide your decisions today? Whether it's the memory of overcoming a personal obstacle, the insight gained from a difficult conversation, or the quiet strength you discovered during a time of adversity, these experiences form the soundtrack of your resilience. Embrace these echoes as a reminder that every experience, no matter how challenging, contributes to the masterpiece of your life.

PRACTICAL EXERCISES: HARNESSING THE ECHOES

1. **Reflective Listening**: Spend a few minutes each evening in quiet reflection. Allow yourself to recall a recent challenge or triumph and listen to what it teaches you. Write down any insights or recurring themes that emerge.
2. **Share Your Story**: Initiate a conversation with someone who may be struggling. Share a piece of your journey and ask them to reflect on a similar experience in their life. Notice how the conversation reinforces the strength that lies within both of you.

3. **Mindful Reminders**: Create a small token or a visual reminder—a piece of jewelry, a photo, or even a written note—that symbolizes your journey. Place it somewhere you can see it daily to remind you of the inner echoes that guide your decisions and fuel your growth.

AFFIRMATION

"The echoes of my journey resonate within me, guiding every step I take. I carry the wisdom of my past in my heart, using it to forge a future filled with hope, strength, and purpose."

CLOSING REFLECTION

The journey may have ended on the physical plane, but its echoes live on—transforming ordinary moments into extraordinary reminders of our potential. As you move forward, let these resonances inspire you to face new challenges with the same courage and conviction that carried you through your most daunting moments. In every heartbeat, in every quiet pause, there lies a reminder of your strength and the limitless possibilities that await. Embrace these echoes, for they are the silent legacy of every challenge overcome and every victory earned on the bridge within.

Ram Setu Swim Expedition

A 32 KM swim expedition from Sri Lanka to India by Shaaswat & Bharat

A token contribution for Universal Brotherhood and friendship between neighbors"

April 14, 2024

SHAASWAT SHARMA

A NATIONAL LEVEL SWIMMER, WATERPOLO PLAYER, TRIATHLETE AND ULTRA LONG-DISTANCE SWIMMER, WITH OVER 500 MEDALS, AWARDS AND TROPHIES

@shaaswat.sharma

BHARAT SACHDEVA

AN INTERNATIONAL SWIMMER IRONMAN TRIATHLETE, HIGH PERFORMANCE HEALTH AND WELLNESS CONSULTANT WITH NUMEROUS MEDALS AT NATIONAL AND INTERNATIONAL LEVEL

@thewarrior.yogi

www.ingramcontent.com/pod-product-compliance
Lightning Source LLC
Chambersburg PA
CBHW072048150726
47996CB00015B/2185